NATURE'S QUIET WISDOM

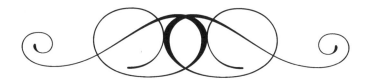

LYNN H. WYVILL

© 2019 Lynn H. Wyvill

Nature's Quiet Wisdom
First Edition, August 2019

Publisher: Lynn H. Wyvill
Fredericksburg, Virginia
LynnHWyvill.com

Editing: Stacia Fleegal
Proofreading: Shayla Raquel, ShaylaRaquel.com
Cover Design & Interior Formatting: Melinda Martin, MelindaMartin.me
Photography: John Berry
Cover Art: Richard F. Wyvill

ISBN: 978-1-7333545-0-9 (paperback)

To my husband, Richard

To Andi,
May you always
enjoy nature's peace!

Lynn H. Wyrill

Contents

JOY

PEACE

HOLD HANDS

We clutch cell phones in our hands, captivated by all they offer us. We never want to take our eyes from them, never want to be without them. We are consumed by our love for them.

This obsession isn't healthy. Our bodies and minds are worn out. Our senses are numb. We are missing so much that no cell phone can give us.

If we never look away from our phones, we won't see the tree frog hiding in a carpet of fallen leaves.

If we don't take off our headphones, we'll never hear the rain falling.

If we never seek refuge in nature, we'll never find the peace that the Canadian geese enjoy when they fold their ecru wings against their bodies and rest quietly in the shade.

Without nature, our spirits become like a decayed hole in the base of an old tree that still lives but is missing a piece of its heart.

Nature wants to hold our hand for a short walk in a city park or a day along a wooded trail or a weekend by the water. "Spend time with me," nature beckons. She says, "I will wipe away stress that rests as heavy as boulders and turn them into skipping stones you can cast into a lake's deep water."

"Spend time with me," nature says, "so your mind can freely wander like clouds drifting in a delicate blue sky."

Only then will we gather our own thoughts, as plentiful as

wildflowers, which no amount of staring at a screen could ever conjure.

KISSED WITH RED

I come from a world where car horns blare, bus exhaust sullies the air, and the chaos of life weighs heavily like a sultry summer day.

Eager to escape that world, I seek peace on a walk along a canal where tiny turtles sit alone, one per small stump. Big turtles gather for an afternoon nap on tree trunks that have toppled into the water. Their stillness interrupted by the occasional stretch of their necks or a slight twitch of a foot. Maybe they are dreaming.

A long, tapered leaf wiggles in the water. "I have something to show you," it says. It points to a fish with a luminous aqua-blue tail that swims around a school of smaller fish lined up like children in their classroom desks.

What is today's lesson? I wonder.

Across the canal, a turtle climbs out of the water to sunbathe on a fallen tree trunk.

In his stillness, I notice something unexpected. The edge of his dark-green shell is kissed with red.

I wonder if the turtle knows it's there. I hope he feels it pulse through him like a scarlet vein in a deep-green leaf.

In my stillness, I think about my own kiss of red on the edge of my shell and begin to feel its pulse beat within me.

A dragonfly with a slender teal body and gossamer black-and-white-striped wings stops and asks me to dance with him.

Gift of Days

Waves curve like a cupped hand far from shore before relaxing into a smooth watery palm as they reach the beach. They whisper good morning as they offer their treasure of rocks and shells in a delicate froth at my feet.

They come laden with my favorites: pink, lavender, and amethyst shells.

"All for me?" I ask as the ocean picks up her lacy skirt and runs back out to sea to gather more gifts for me.

The sun beams as the tireless ocean flows back and forth, bestowing on me yellow, charcoal, bronze, and bright-white beauties all tumbled together like candy in a glass bowl.

My hands can't hold all that the ocean gives me, but how can I refuse?

In the salty skim of water, the shells rest soft in my hands. My fingers trace the irresistible bumpy, ridged, and ragged ones. I stroke the glossy flat shells and explore the bowl and spiral-shaped ones. I hold up the translucent and iridescent shells to shimmer in the hot white sunshine.

Around my feet are rough shells with sharp, jagged edges that poke and cut into my skin. I ask the sea to take them away where time and salt water will wear them smooth.

Our days are like these shells. Some are smooth, others rough. Some are wildly colorful, and others are comforting and quiet. We endure fragile days and gratefully accept days of strength. We cling to those that delight and ask that the painful ones be wiped away.

All days are gifts from God. I know that because I found a shell marked with His soft purple thumbprint.

Morning's Light

I rise just before dawn and sit quietly under the night sky. Cold, clean air brushes away sleep's fog as I wait for dawn.

This is when I pray, searching for words to say what is deep in my heart.

When I have poured out my soul, I rest in this sacred peace.

The sun tiptoes in and slowly opens the shade. Morning light peeks over the horizon as the sky awakens.

The sun streams through the sky's stained-glass windows. Hopeful yellow, tender loving pink, and peaceful lavender light up the day.

Feathery clouds float across the sky like angels' wings. They bear understanding that can be found only in stillness, knowledge that can be heard only in silence. And God sends wisdom for the path forward.

LIVE IN PEACE

I was hiking not long ago and found what I thought was a frayed black-and-white rope resting on a large, flat rock in the sun. When I took a closer look, I discovered it wasn't a rope, but the spine, bones, and some skin of a snake.

It looked like it had just curled up peacefully and died.

I thought about a snake's life. A snake sheds its skin when its body outgrows its old one and a new brighter self emerges.

Can we grow if we don't shed our old selves so better ones can emerge?

How do we live so we can die in peace? I wondered as a solitary turtle swam below the surface of the river.

WISDOM OF THE GULLS

Ashy gray clouds splotch the sky.

Rough, slate-gray ocean waves roll and crash in a temper tantrum of foamy fury.

The angry wind scrapes up sand and dumps it on stairs, benches, and sidewalks. In its rage, it flings sand at people and declares, "I'll go where I want and do what I please. You cannot stop me."

The gulls and I stubbornly fight the wind. The gulls stiffen their wings and pull their necks into their bodies as they struggle to fly. I hunch my shoulders, tuck my head down, and lean into the wind. Sand stings my face with sharp pricks, making it difficult to see.

The wind fights back, growling and shoving us everywhere we don't want to go. The more we resist, the more forceful the wind becomes.

Tired of the battle, the gulls spread their wings and stretch their bodies long and fly with the wind. I put the wind at my back.

With no one to fight, the wind calms to a breeze. The sky softens to light blue. The sea relaxes into gentle waves, lapping at my feet as I walk and the gulls soar overhead.

WALK IN THE WOODS

Life's demands felt like heavy rocks piled up along a mountain path. My thoughts darted around like a scurry of chipmunks that couldn't decide which way to run.

I was worn out and desperately needed to be alone for a while.

I found a path by a small stream and set out for a walk in the cool fall air. Turns out I wasn't the only one who needed some solitude.

A caterpillar, bundled up in a fuzzy orange-and-brown-striped suit, black hat, and boots, strolled by.

One small bird wove through the trees and then hid in the brush. A doe tiptoed through grass and paused, watching to make sure I wouldn't bother her. A crinkly dry leaf drifted lazily to the ground, avoiding an ant wandering by. A stream drifted past rocks.

The leaves, however, wanted company, so they hitched a ride on the stream. The water didn't mind as long as they were quiet.

I, too, had picked up a hitchhiker; a tiny bright-green worm clung to my jacket. I was ready for some company.

As we happily traveled together in silence, we noticed others gathered together. Under my feet, fallen leaves arranged themselves into a luxurious rug. They covered the gravel and soil that bonded together to create a path. Overhead, leaves wove a canopy to shade me. Hundreds of jagged rocks packed themselves together to form a strong wall.

My green friend and I traveled together for a long time. And when we were ready to walk solo again, we parted ways.

A bit of sun peeked through and shone on the trees where vines grew, clinging to rough bark. Crisscrossing the trunks, the vines touched each other, then didn't touch, but they never climbed very far apart.

A Winter's Pause

Winter strips the landscape to its bare bones. Chill, damp air announces that short days and long darkness will soon be here. Animals curl up and sleep.

What if we did that?

What would we find in ourselves if we stripped away everything to the bare bones of our lives for a while and rested in silence?

What if we spent a little time alone with only the sound of our breathing for company?

Then, we could hear the hush of snow falling.

What if we paused in peace so our rushing, pounding blood could flow calmly?

Then, we'd notice the tiniest snowflakes twirl from the pale-blue sky.

What if we burrowed beneath the crust of ourselves that the world sees to explore who we are and what we want to be?

Then, our depleted selves could recharge and emerge refreshed like spring's tulips.

JUST BE

The garden soil lies anxious but silent. Its cycle of planting, growing, and yielding suspended.

"What should I do now?" the ground whispers impatiently.

"Rest," Mother Nature answers.

"Just stop? Are you kidding? I'm used to working hard, long hours," the soil replies.

Mother Nature smiles. "I know, but you're exhausted."

The ground sighs. "I can't rest."

"Yes, you can," Mother Nature says. "Over the next year, I will send the sun to warm your heart, the moon to watch over you, the rains to sing lullabies, and the snow to blanket you."

"But then what? I'd like to know," the ground moans.

"Hush and don't worry," she says. "In time, tiny seeds will fall into your contours once again, sprouting a new garden that will flourish where the old one once grew."

"But why must I rest for a year? I'm sure I can blossom now, if I just work harder," the soil protests.

Mother Nature chuckles. "Be patient and take the time you're being given. You will grow strong and blossom into something unlike anything you've ever been before."

BLISS

The gulls waited patiently for ocean waves to deliver sand crabs on the shore. When their meal appeared, they raced on skinny legs to grab it before it disappeared under a blanket of wet sand.

There was one seagull, however, that skipped the seaside buffet. He knew something better than gritty snack-size morsels awaited him. His patience paid off. He won the lunchtime lottery — a long, thick, golden-brown pizza crust. He strutted down the boardwalk with that crust held tight in his beak, as proud of himself as a kid who has just learned to tie his shoes.

Despite his accomplishment, the gull didn't want the other birds to discover his secret. He knew if they found out, they would swoop down on him, squawking, badgering, and grabbing until they wrestled the crust away from him.

But for now, he wasn't going to worry about anything. Not the other gulls. Not if he had bitten off more than he could chew. Not calories or carbs.

In this glorious moment, he found a secluded picnic spot in the sun, felt the ocean breeze ruffle his feathers, and savored his delicious seaside lunch.

Life's Seasons

The transition between the seasons is never smooth.

The other day, I woke up to winter, and by afternoon, it was spring. Should I wear my heavy coat when I leave the house and carry it with me the rest of the day? Or should I wear a light sweater and freeze in the morning to be comfortable in the afternoon?

Guessing what season you are in is frustrating. It reminds me of childhood when one minute I'd hear, "You're too old for that." Only to be told later the same day, "You're too young for that."

Was I young or old? Was it possible to be both at the same time?

I'm wrestling with the same question again. Am I young or am I old?

I bounce from being spring, bursting with enthusiasm for new ideas, to being summer, a bit wiser and more relaxed. Then I am autumn, bold and energetic, before I slip into my winter self to savor the pleasures of this wondrous life.

An Abundant Life

We came as spring's young buds that blinked open in the warm sunlight. We blossomed into tender green leaves that fluttered in the breeze as we cradled robins' nests. We played hide-and-seek with kites and birthday balloons.

In summer, we grew into dark-green leaves that danced in the rain and basked in the hot sun. We threw parties where mockingbirds sang and woodpeckers feasted. We spread ourselves into thick canopies under which people read for hours, families picnicked, and lovers kissed.

We thought we'd always be young and strong. Our lush abundance fooled us into believing we would live forever. Then change crept up on us and caught us unprepared.

We are different now than we were in our youth but still boldly beautiful. As we grow into old age, our brilliant crimson, fiery orange, and bright-gold colors are proof that life is far from over. Squirrels play among us as lovers walk hand in hand beneath our colorful tent. We mound ourselves into fluffy piles for giggling children.

But our days will grow shorter. We will dance more slowly under a cooler sun and tremble in the wind. We'll shiver in the chilly rain until a frosty gust places us gently on the ground. Eventually, we'll turn to dust and drift away on the whispered breath of an icy breeze, hoping someone will remember our colorful seasons when the next tender green appears.

Wishing upon a Birdbath

The thermometer is stuck at 20 degrees. It's been that way for far too long. The experts say it's one degree warmer today than yesterday, but I can't feel it.

A sparrow sits on a birdbath that's been turned upside down so it won't freeze and crack. We're both hoping spring will come soon.

Maybe I can coax tulips, daffodils, and crocus bulbs to bloom by gazing longingly at the place where they rest in the cold soil.

Perhaps if I sit in a lawn chair wearing sandals and shorts and stare at the covered swimming pool, I can charm the sun to shine brighter.

I could sit on an upside-down birdbath, even hold my breath, but I can't persuade spring to come out of hiding. Like the sparrow, I must be patient until winter's stubborn self is ready to go away.

NOT YET

The magnolia tree took its time blooming this year. My heart beat faster when I noticed the first tender green sprouts on its slender branches. *Surely, magnolia blossoms can't be far behind,* I thought.

But the tree whispered, "Not yet."

Each morning, I checked, hoping the tree had burst into magnificent blooms. But the magnolia would not be rushed.

Finally, one day, hundreds of thick, smoky-green buds covered the branches. They plumped up under the warm sun and grew so enormous that I thought they'd burst right before my eyes.

But they didn't.

"How long will you make me wait?" I asked.

The magnolia murmured, "Not long."

"Please hurry," I pleaded. Waiting for spring's rosy color to peek out of those expectant buds and burst open was like anticipating my birthday when I was five.

Then one morning, the magnolia greeted me with huge flowers of creamy vanilla and purple-pink petals as soft as a baby's cheeks. They enveloped the branches so completely, I could not see the tree's body beneath.

I spent as much time with my beautiful blossoms as I could. The flowers lasted only a few days. Slowly, the magnolia began its gentle shower of falling petals, dropping its springtime coat over its roots. Too soon, that cloak of pink, white, and lavender turned a deerskin brown and began withering away.

"Not yet," I begged the magnolia tree.

"I'll see you next spring," the tree promised.

QUIET TIME

The bright-red sign with big letters commands me to STOP. The car is still, but my brain isn't.

So I park and retreat to a porch overlooking a river. I close my eyes and tilt my face toward the sun and enjoy the kaleidoscope of colors playing on my eyelids. My shoulders relax, and my thoughts melt like ice on a warm day.

In the quiet, I hear crickets hum. I listen to the soft *ting-ting-ting* of a wind chime as tree limbs dance in the breeze without disturbing a single leaf.

The day slips quietly toward dusk. All God's creation settles down to stillness.

Peach, pink, and gold light peeks through the curtain of low, puffy clouds.

The river smooths its wrinkled face and so do I, as all worries are washed away.

The birds' twitters sing a lullaby as the earth's eyelids flutter closed and the day pulls the shade of night gently down.

THE DAILY RACE

Sandpipers race on spindly legs to catch tiny sand crabs before waves bury their dinner. Usually, they don't get much more than a nibble of seafood at a time. I wonder if they get discouraged.

I do sometimes. Most days, I run back and forth trying to keep up with an endless list of chores. It seems that no matter how many items I cross off, relentless waves of time always bring more to do.

As I stand in the surf, the sea casts a spell over me. I forget everything as the water washes over my feet. Sand clings to my legs and won't let go. I watch dolphins slip through the water, swimming slow and steady, enjoying the wash of the waves over their backs. Pelicans skim the water in their leisurely flight, dipping their wings and beaks into the swells.

Sandpipers dash to and from the sea, but I vow to never rush again.

NEW DAY

The early morning sun lights the tips of clouds like golden points on meringue.

The tips of the ocean's waves are shimmering crystal shards.

Sand crabs scurry across the beach and dive into the sand as it quickly shifts and covers their tracks. The gulls wait in the wet sand for a wave, but when it comes, they skitter away like shy children to their mothers.

The gulls' feet make the first tracks on the beach. Other footprints soon appear, some large and heavy, others light and delicate, baby steps, running-shoe steps, in-a-hurry steps, all-the-time-in-the-world steps.

The ocean stands back like a parent watching the tentative toddling of a child, leaving our footsteps, sandcastles, and love messages untouched.

Frothy waves dance in the briny breeze and dissolve as the day's minutes slip by. The salty water bears smooth shells that sit soft and silky in my hand. It also carries sharp, jagged ones that are too rough to handle, and I ask the sea to take them away.

The ocean comes and goes. Dolphins swim, cradled in the water as I was cradled in my mother's womb, as I am cradled in God's arms. Darkness descends and brings with it, sleep.

At dawn, the ocean sweeps in with its gift of smooth sand on which to write a new day.

LOVE

Ramble and Rush

The stream hums a sweet song for the trees that stand along its banks.

When it meets rocks, the water gurgles a quick hello and continues on its way.

The stream stops to chat for a while with piles of leaves. Sometimes, the leaves join the stream on its stroll, content to let the water decide which way they will go. When the leaves tire, they rest along the banks and the stream hurries off, as if late for a very important appointment.

Fish join the rushing stream, wiggling here and there, before they race ahead like eager children and ask, "When are we going to get there?" The water laughs as it rushes to catch up.

The stream rambles when it wants to, rushes when it needs to, but never stands still. Where would it go, who would it meet, and who would it help if it just stopped moving?

Always in Season

In spring, Mother Nature wears a dazzling chartreuse suit. Plum petals cover her hat, and she bedecks herself with amethyst tulip jewelry. We run outside to show her our new spring clothes, pretty pink dresses, straw hats, and navy suits.

In summer, Mother Nature wears a grass-green sarong. She tucks pink peonies behind her ears and weaves yellow daisies into bracelets. We rest beside her in cutoff shorts, soft T-shirts, and bathing suits.

In autumn, Mother Nature colors her cheeks crimson and dons dangling acorn earrings, an orange cap, and bronze slippers. We beg her to color our cheeks rosy red.

When the snow falls, she wraps herself in a white hat and cloak that glisten in the sun and glow in the moonlight. Her jewels are red berries and crystal icicles. We bundle ourselves into downy coats and make angels in the snow.

In every season, we're all beautiful on the outside no matter what we wear.

But what about our inner beauty? What will our hearts wear all year long, no matter the season? Wouldn't we look marvelous clothed year-round in the gentle fabric of kindness? Wouldn't we look lovely in the cool cloth of patience embroidered with love and understanding?

Love at the Pond

A grassy slope leads me to the pond. Ripples skip across the water to meet me and cattails wave hello. A shy frog hiding nearby croaks once to begin a welcoming chorus that he and his friends sing for me.

The grass around the pond is dotted with yellow buttercups, scattered here and there. Those clustered close to the water are the happiest.

We're just alike, these flowers and me. So I settle myself on a nearby hammock, place one foot on the ground, and slowly rock.

A spruce tree watches over the pond and me. At the touch of its tender lime-green fingertips, a pine tree sighs a fragrant breath. They are in love.

Two geese stand in the tall grass at the far end of the pond, facing each other, bill to bill, so close they can kiss. Maybe they do, but the shy lovers hide and won't let me see.

Others want to show off for me. A fish leaps, a flash of wet, white belly glittering in the sun. A sparrow sings and geese land, sending echoing rings across the pond. The bees dance together with the butterflies in a graceful ballet.

Some don't want to share the pond with me. An ant crawls over my feet and bites me, urging me to move on. I move my feet out of his way, but I am staying. Annoyed, the ant marches back home.

Thunder rumbles in the distance, and the sky turns an ominous steel blue. "I'm not leaving," I tell them, so they slip away.

Geese take off as their wings raise splashes in quick succession, like the dot and dash of a coded message. "We must go," they say, "but you must stay."

I do, happily rocking in the hammock by the pond I love, surrounded by buttercups.

ROBIN CASANOVA

A robin sits on the fence outside the kitchen window. He stares at me while I stare at him.

He puffs his red breast up until it looks like it might pop, macho and proud. His eyes are deep dark pools edged in white. His tail feathers fold right over left to create the top curves of a Valentine heart.

My robe is rumpled, and my hair tangled. My bare face is pale and creased from sleep. But my dark eyes are smiling at him.

Are we falling in love?

He stays awhile longer but shifts from one foot to the other, anxious to be on his way. As he goes, he glances at me one more time before he flies off.

I'm worried. Is he playing hard to get? Does he flirt with other women?

I try to forget him. But the next morning, there he is waiting for me outside the window. We flirt a little while, and then he flies away. Again.

My robin appears every time I open the blinds, pass a window, or leave the house. He stands on the mulch and protects the garden like a lifeguard on a beach. Then he flies to the porch roof and surveys his valley kingdom to ensure all is well.

Satisfied, he sits on the chain-link fence and lifts one wing and then the other, grooming himself handsome, just for me. He fluffs up his feathers and serenades me. When he is finished, I talk to him. He listens attentively, nods, and agrees with everything I say.

Date with the Dolphins

We have a date, same time, same place every year. But this year you, my dolphin friends, kept me waiting.

Where were you?

I stood on the beach, looking right and left, waiting for you, eager to be with you since we have only one week a year together. But you didn't appear.

I can forgive the first day. Maybe you just didn't feel like being out when it was chilly and overcast.

The second day, I saw your pelican friends. But no sign of you. Then the rain came, and I knew I wouldn't see you that day, either.

On the third day, I caught a glimpse of you as you rushed by, in a hurry to see someone else, I suppose.

I have to tell you, I was hurt and disappointed.

Finally, on the fourth day, when I had just about given up, all of you stopped to see me. I was so happy and you must have felt the same way because you jumped clear out of the waves. Your fins popped in and out of the ocean as you swam laps, as pelicans skimmed the water.

You hung out with me the whole day.

I haven't seen you today. Maybe you're tired from our party yesterday.

Even though I wish we had spent all week together, I forgive you.

A LOVE STORY

When his gorgeous, big, bright eyes met mine, I fell in love. His gleaming grass-green skin looked like he had been waxed and buffed to a shine. His feet were too large for the rest of his two-inch body. What a handsome guy!

I found my new sweetheart, an American tree frog, clinging to the front tire of my car in an urban shopping center parking lot.

Was he someone's pet that had jumped out of the aquarium, took advantage of open doors, and hopped off to the local shopping center? Did he come from a nearby creek? Did he cross that wide road where heavy traffic never stops?

Was his tiny heart beating with excitement or fear as he traveled solo in the land of human giants, bravely exploring a dangerous world?

Even though he seemed to be enjoying his great adventure, my little friend couldn't stay here. When I offered an outstretched hand, he eagerly climbed aboard. Wrapped in a warm embrace, he held on tight and poked his green head out to make sure he saw all the wonderful sights.

Despite my love for him, I had to let him go. He loved me too—I could tell. But he needed to be free. I found some tall grass and shredded bark, and we said a sad goodbye. Then my happy, brave little frog hopped off to continue his adventure.

Funny Friend

Trees welcome autumn, turning green leaves gold, crimson, and copper. Out of the hundreds, a leaf—bright as a lemon and shaped like a hand—catches my eye. On it, Mother Nature has drawn a face with two playful ebony eyes.

Each time I pass the kitchen window, my new leaf friend waves at me with an enthusiastic, cheerful up and down, up and down.

"Hello, hello," I imagine it saying. "I'm so glad to see you." When the breeze blows, the leaf makes funny faces at me, and I laugh aloud.

The rest of the leaves sway in the cool, crisp air, but their dance doesn't last long. They take just a few twirls before they fall to the ground.

Just as I am marveling that my yellow leaf is still with me, a stiff breeze plucks it from its home and sends it tumbling. In the snap of the fingers, it's gone. Gone! I have lost my sunny, funny friend.

Now cool, damp air creeps in where my yellow leaf had been just seconds ago. I stare at the vacant space and wonder if anyone besides me noticed this happy gold leaf while it lived.

BROKEN HEARTS

The pond and the pine tree have been best friends forever. I haven't known them long, but I loved them at first sight.

Long ago, the pine's trunk forked into three thick branches. Two shaded the ground while the third one stretched over the pond.

I wasn't there when it happened, but something — wind, old age, or maybe both — ripped the pine tree in two. The branch stretched over the water, broke, and collapsed into the arms of the pond. The living tree, its splintered heart exposed, stared in disbelief at its loss.

The living and the dying clung to each other, like lovers in one last goodbye embrace. A trail of silent resin tears hung from the rough bark of the one left behind. The grass at its feet quivered like lips fighting back sobs.

The funereal crape of brittle brown pine needles draped itself over the grieving one. Empty spiderwebs shrouded the small dark hollow in the tree's trunk. Private memories of its beloved rest here, held close for the tree and no one else.

Ants guarded this sacred space, nipping at my bare feet, hoping I would move on. But I couldn't. My mourning, and that of all who loved the tree, was not over.

The pond flowed around the dying branch, comforting it with its cool touch. Shimmering ripples flickered on the bare limbs, like an old movie of their life together.

Frogs sang in deep baritone as pine boughs nodded in a breeze. Birds flew low and slow through the branches. Black-

and-white dragonflies hovered close by. The sun hugged all of us.

I gently touched the nubby skin of the pine to let it know I was there.

THE MIGHTY OAK

I didn't see the massive oak start life, but I witnessed its old age. There was no birth certificate, but based on the size of the trunk, I'd guess it was at least 200 years old.

Each year, the oak blossomed with yellow-green leaves that matured to a deep green in summer and turned to russet foliage in the fall.

It was a tough old tree, dressed in armor of coarse bark, daring insects, scrapes, and disease to come near. Thunderstorms and heat, even a hurricane, didn't bother it. The oak didn't care about standing naked in freezing temperatures or being coated with ice. Its heavy limbs welcomed snow, like children sticking out their tongues to catch drifting flakes.

But one calm, sunny summer day, when we least expected it, there was a sickening thud. One of the oak's enormous branches broke off, smashed a picnic table, and left a deep gouge in the ground.

No one was hurt, but the oak was. We hoped it would survive, but the loss was too much. The mighty oak died and had to be cut down.

In the weeks afterward, in the first groggy moments of morning, I would glance out the kitchen window expecting the oak tree to be there, standing tall.

Months went by until one day, instead of loss, I saw something else. Where the tree had been, now I could see the earth's blue-and-white cathedral ceiling welcoming me into the day.

Now I watch the birds splash in basins of cool water and flutter to feeders to collect seeds. I see squirrels perform their acrobatics, snatching treats like children sneaking cookies before dinner.

But my heart still aches from the loss of the mighty oak.

Grandma's Girl

The low, sturdy stone wall where I sit still holds the warmth of the sun, now hiding behind the gray clouds. Far away, thunder grumbles under its breath. The sky bulges, ready to burst with rain.

When it does come, it's so light I can't see it, but I can feel every single drop lightly tap my back.

A breeze carries the faint scent of a boxwood hedge, just like the ones that surrounded my grandma's house. It brings with it tender memories of how she stopped everything to listen to every silly thing I had to say and didn't mind if I woke her up early just to be with her.

Her house was very different from our house. Everything was softer—the colors on the wall, the overstuffed sofa, and the chime of the doorbell. The place I loved the most was the kitchen with its old-fashioned appliances and huge porcelain farm sink. I remember the first time I was alone in that room and discovered a hidden treasure behind a worn wooden cupboard door. I could barely reach the black snap latch, but when I did, I found a butter dish containing the softest, creamiest yellow butter I had ever seen.

I knew I didn't have to ask, so I slathered some on a slice of velvety white bread and took a bite. The flavors melded together and bathed my tongue in salty, sweet, yeasty perfection. And then I made another, the butter thicker and heavier.

As I ate, I stared out the window at the huge oak trees that shaded the backyard and listened to the murmuring conversation of the grown-ups. When I was done, I found Grandma and climbed into her arms for a nap.

My memories of Grandma come like small white butterflies that play as the breeze runs its gentle fingertips over the creek's green grass.

GRACE

The pale-blue sky glowed with the radiant late-afternoon sun like millions of votive candles illuminating an altar. Mounds of whipped-cream-like clouds sprinkled with gold and rimmed in silver floated in the heavens. But a special cloud shone brighter than any other one in the sky and captured my heart.

The wispy cloud formed a little girl's innocent face. This darling child with an upturned nose, chubby cheeks, and bright eyes lifted her face to heaven. The cap perched on the back of her head, trailed off into a pointy end as she joyfully ran in the wind. I'm sure she was giggling as she played in the heavens, even though I was not close enough to hear.

As the cloud shifted, I saw that she held a tiny bird in her cupped hands. Even though this treasure, which I'm sure she deeply loved, was everything she had, she wouldn't keep it. Instead, she lifted her plump baby arms and offered her precious gift to me. Her face beamed as I accepted it.

Was the sky so bright because of the sun or because of this little girl in the clouds? This glorious, golden light could have only come from this luminescent girl's joyful, pure heart. Without her, the world would not have been as bright.

A Butterfly Feast

Zinnias popped up from seeds. They grew into a tall table loaded with a delicious buffet of juicy flowers for birds, bees, and butterflies.

A bee choses a pink zinnia and feasts until the flower is dry. Then it stands on its back legs and stretches. Deciding its belly isn't full yet, it moves to a yellow zinnia.

Hummingbirds come too, but all they want to do is gulp a quick snack and be on their way. The goldfinches are picky eaters. Like a child picking peas he doesn't like out of a casserole, the goldfinches pluck the petals off the flowers to find the seeds they do love.

Butterflies sit on the brightest blooms, stick their tongues into the succulent flowers, and suck the sweet nectar. They take their time to dine leisurely, moving from one flower to the next. Unable to contain their enjoyment, their wings beat rhythmically, up and down as they eat.

A turquoise butterfly arrives and can't decide what to sample first; there are so many luscious choices. Two dainty butterflies greet each other like old friends meeting for coffee before settling at their orange zinnia table. A butterfly mom brings a little one to enjoy a snack.

As I stand near the flowers, a butterfly dances around me. She graciously moves to the end of the garden and invites me to share the zinnia feast.

LOVE'S TOKEN

A wooden pier juts into the river, its wood bearing the initials of lovers and a name, Abby. On this altar to love, a small hinged clam shell rests on its side. In the opening is an offering of some soil, a twig, and dried sea grass.

I wonder why it's here. Maybe someone found it along the river's muddy shore and accidentally left it behind. Maybe someone created it as a token of love.

Were they too shy to offer their gift? Was it offered and refused? I hope it was left here because it was forgotten in the enthusiasm of an embrace and the tenderness of a kiss.

It's sad that most will never see love's token. Those who never come to the river, those who never walk on the pier, those who do but don't notice.

I'd like to take this gift home, but I won't. I'll leave it for whomever comes after me, a reminder to never overlook, ignore, or reject love.

COURAGE

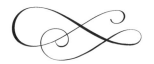

CREATING ME

There is one lake nestled among low mountains that has a special place in my heart. It's my refuge where I can meditate about big questions whose answers elude me as if trying to catch a fish with my bare hands.

I've come today with a question I've been struggling with for a long time.

Who am I?

A strange question, given my age.

I know who I have been. Ever since I was a child, I followed a script written by others. My life has been full of what others wanted, even demanded. A good life, but one too full of other people's dreams instead of my own.

So who am I, really?

I wonder if now is the time to realize long-delayed dreams, or is this the time for brand-new ones, never imagined before?

The insects that buzz overhead share my excitement about my future. I think about what will bring me contentment as I watch curious deer peacefully explore the lakeshore. I listen to frogs croak in their unique voices, and I know I will find mine. I will fly free like birds. Just like clouds, I will form and re-form into anything I want to be.

As I daydream about the "me" of my own creation, the cool cradle of the lake rocks me, a baby on the cusp of new life.

SHOOTING PAST ROCKS

I've always been fascinated by trees that spring up between boulders. How do their seeds get there and take root?

Their births must be difficult as they squeeze through narrow crevices between massive rocks and then stretch, bend, and find the sun. While they have no choice about how wide they can be, they can decide how high they will grow and how lush they will become.

Their journey is much like our own. We are born through a narrow canal and struggle. We bend and stretch to reach for opportunities as plentiful as the leaves on trees. We embrace the possible, as well as the improbable, as we shoot up past the rocky obstacles in our paths. The heights we achieve and the lushness of our lives are up to us.

DEEP POOLS

My backyard is a playground for the birds. They play hide-and-seek among the azaleas and oaks. When they're hot and sweaty, they head to a shallow birdbath.

There are never more than two birds at a time in the pool, and there is always a line to get in. Some wait patiently on the garden shed roof. Others hop from one foot to the other on the lawn, eager for their turn. When they finally do jump in, they joyfully splash, flap, and dunk their heads.

They could go to the other birdbath, which is larger and deeper, but some of the birds are afraid to use it. A few adventurous ones approach it cautiously. They circle the rim, debating with themselves about whether they should jump in. They tell themselves they're brave, but they don't quite believe it.

They stare at the water as they gather their courage, and take a quick hop in and out before returning to their safe perch. They may wonder what they were so nervous about. Nothing awful happened. Maybe they enjoyed it. Perhaps, it was even thrilling. They swear they'll jump in again. Later. Perhaps.

Shallow pools are easy, safe choices, but deep pools, filled with risk and uncertainty, are frightening. And yet, they beckon us to be brave.

LOVE'S PULSE

As soon as I heard the river's rush, I hurried to meet it.

The river opened its arms and said, "Please come in. I'm so glad you're here."

I took off my shoes and stood at the river's doorway. Even though it was an intensely hot day, the brisk cold water greeted me with a shock. I hesitated to wade in.

A yellow-and-black butterfly danced around my head. "Don't just stand there—jump in," it said. I climbed over slippery rocks and found a comfortable place to sit. The boulder in the middle of the river was flat and dry and warmed by the sun, the perfect spot to enjoy the river's company.

Along the water's edge, white-and-yellow trumpet vases filled with the honeysuckle's sweetness twined around tall shade trees, like lovers who can't keep their hands off each other. Not wanting to be left out, chubby bushes laden with cuplike bright-white flowers hugged them all.

Sunlight filtered through the leaves and kissed my skin. Cool air brushed my hair. The gnarled, tangled roots of the old trees that lined the banks felt it too.

The river's heart thumped with the same excitement that beat in my chest and pulsed through the trees' bare roots.

Butterfly Guide

I'm barreling down the interstate of life, lost and low on fuel. My mind and body are carrying on like two cranky kids in the back seat of a car. So in the interest of keeping the peace, I stop and let them out to play on a mountain trail. The well-marked path requires nothing more than putting one foot in front of the other.

When I reach the peak, peace wraps herself around me. Silence sits beside me.

The sun's thousand votive candles light up the summer sky. Leafy oak trees are the acolytes for trees that lift their bleached bare limbs to heaven in prayer.

I pray too.

"Show me the way," I plead.

As I walk back down the mountain, I meet a butterfly that flutters her delicate royal-blue wings as she hovers in front of me. When she is certain that I will follow her, she flies ahead. The butterfly perches on a stone and waits patiently for me to catch up. When I do, she flies ahead again.

The butterfly is the promise that there will always be a guide out of the brambles of fear and tangled vines of doubt on life's steep rocky trail.

STONE FACE

I was strolling along the beach when the funniest looking rock I had ever seen caught my eye. A man's face was carved on its quarter-size surface.

His craggy features were a mystery. His left side grinned at me while his right side twisted in pain. A deep gouge ran past his bulbous nose, wrapped itself under his chin, and crept up the back of his skull. At the end of this trail of sadness were two tiny holes.

I tipped him on his side, hoping that some of his wisdom would trickle into my hand.

"Wisdom is earned," he said. "It can be found in your heart where the pleasure and pain of your life is written."

Our Compost Pile

After months of freezing temperatures, we rush outdoors blinking in the warm, bright spring light. Enthusiastically, we rake, prune, and yank the tired, overgrown, and unwanted from our gardens and lawns.

Some of it ends up in the trash can, but some of it is composted. We toss grass clippings, twigs, dead leaves, vines, and flowers into bins discreetly tucked away. Water binds it together; the sun's heat bakes it. Bugs and worms join in to move the decomposition along.

From time to time, we turn the pile. Each pitchfork full of the moist muck is moved so the top becomes the bottom, the bottom becomes the top. This damp pile softens and blends into a mass of rich, earthy nutrients to spread over the garden for the next growing season.

Everyone has a compost pile.

Not one in a yard, but a secret pile of memories at the back of our minds that we don't want to think about. We rake up disappointments and trim relationships that no longer work. We sweep mistakes into a pile. We weed out the hurts that choke us.

We throw all of it on our personal compost pile and water it with our tears. The heat of our frustration and anger bakes it.

As much as we'd like to ignore this muck, we turn it over and over, giving it air and light. We dig through the debris, searching for answers and some understanding of ourselves.

We wait patiently as time crumbles this damp brew of flaws,

faults, and failings and blends it together into wisdom. Then we spread it over our lives, and our growing season begins again.

DIFFERENCE OF A DAY

Why are you standing here alone, blue heron? Sleet slices through the air, pummeling your body as a stinging wind rakes your blue-gray feathers. Your feet are anchored to a large patch of ice, one of many formed on the river like scabs on the heart.

That's what we must do sometimes, isn't it? Suffer alone our heartaches. Some are mere pinpricks, others puncture and wound our spirits. Like you, life's storms batter us, and we withstand pain because there is no shelter.

I want to help you but don't know how.

The next day, the air is clean and fresh, scrubbed of yesterday's pain. The scabs of ice are gone. The river is healed like the heart can be. But you are not here.

Did you give up? Did you perish in the storm?

When I've given up hope of seeing you again, here you come out of hiding, gliding past me, wings outstretched, close to the rippling water. Gently, you settle across the river, standing tall, your beautiful feathers smooth across your back. Yesterday gone, but not entirely forgotten, because heartache remembered makes the peace much sweeter.

You rise to fly down the river to visit a friend for a while. Then quietly, you return to me. I walk out on the pier so I can be closer to you. We bask in the winter sun as the water flows tranquilly around us, content being with each other, like two old lovers.

Does the cold breeze brush your feathers as it does my cheek?

Do you hear the squeak of the unseen bird and another's whistle in reply? Do you see the green needles decorated with hundreds of miniature pine cones?

You must, because you are smiling, and so am I.

Steadfast in the Storm

We waited for the storm, huddled in our snug houses. Animals hid in nests and burrows.

Only a broad-winged hawk perched, still and silent, among yellow autumn leaves, fully exposed to the coming storm.

The wind came first, growling, and then intensified to a roar. It beat the hawk's breast, lifting his feathers up and away from his body.

But the hawk was unmoved.

Hard rain arrived, pounding on the roof and pouring down the windows and brick walls. Pearl-size raindrops pressed onto screens and clung for safety. Tree limbs scratched, begging to be let in.

The hawk clutched the bare branch tighter.

The wind flung leaves to the ground and pressed them into soggy layers that stuck to the earth. Gutters caught other leaves and swept them into their swift current until they disappeared down storm drains.

Gradually, the wind subsided and the rain slowed to a shower.

The hawk smoothed his feathers, then silently lifted himself off his perch and flew away.

DUNES

The wind blows billions of grains of sand into dunes. We climb over them, take pictures of them, and sometimes marvel at them.

Mostly, we take them for granted. After all, it's just sand, and there's plenty of that. We believe the dunes will be there forever. But one day, we notice they are smaller than they used to be, worn down by wind and feet.

To save them, we pile them with more sand, plant grass, and put up fences. We ask people to stay off the dunes so we can protect them, so they won't disappear.

Our lives are like the dunes. God's breath blows thousands of seconds into each of our days. Because we believe we'll always have more time, we don't always appreciate the time we do have.

We worry about the past and future instead of enjoying the present. We rush through our days instead of slowing down to savor the sublime. We satisfy others' expectations instead of pursuing what is important to us.

Then one day, we realize how much time has blown away. To protect what is left, we plant our lives with delicate green sprigs of people, places, and pursuits to enjoy under a waning sun.

River Ride

Cautiously, I tiptoe over uneven rocks to the river's bank where I find nature's amusement park.

Shallow pools of water nestle between scattered stones. Black tadpoles wiggle here and there playing. Sturdy, stout water beetles swim quickly among them, racing to see who can get to the finish line first.

Nearby is an empty underwater playground of five flat stones that the aquatic kids haven't discovered yet.

But it's the giant rocky water slide where the river hurries to play.

The timid water chooses a short, gentle kiddie run. It flows lightly over shallow, rocky steps before settling in a calm pool. As it floats there, its ripples echo with a contented sigh.

The more adventurous water wanders left, right, and then left again before finding a deep crevice where it leaps into the air before splashing down.

The wild water hurls itself off the highest rock in an all-at-once, can't-go-fast-enough, exhilarating free fall that ends in a spectacular cannonball. The water laughs and shouts, "Guys, did you see that?"

When they've had enough, all the water gathers for a leisurely float downstream. The bold ones brag about their daredevil feats while the cautious ones wonder if they'll ever be that brave.

STRENGTH

One oak tree stands tall and strong, surrounded by a band of spruce trees. There must have been times through the years when the oak felt small, lonely, and powerless.

Did the spruce trees laugh at the oak as they branched into lush boughs from roots to crowns long before the oak could? Did they mock the oak when it suffered grievous gouges and gashes to its tender, exposed trunk?

Eventually, the oak's wounds scabbed over. Then, the oak armored its body with rough, scaly bark to protect itself.

It took many years for the oak to grow straight and strong. So many that the moss that clings to its bark faded to a powdery pale-green dust.

In that time, the oak remained steadfast and true to itself. It never tried to look or act like the spruce trees. It never became discouraged. It never gave up.

When the oak finally reached an opening, it stretched its limbs wide and burst into abundant green leaves.

Awed by its courage, seven smooth, round, nearly identical rocks gather at its roots. A wild vine climbs over this altar bearing a tribute of a single ripe-red strawberry and touches the oak.

GLISTEN

The small tree bravely stood in the winter rain. The rain was grateful for the tree's company on an icy gray day. As a token of its affection, the rain hung raindrops on every bare branch. The tree accepted as many as it could hold.

Even though the sun could not shine, the sky brightened and the droplets sparkled in the rain.

When our days are cloudy, do we glisten in the light we have?

INNER WILD

I remember Pierre, a fluffy white dog with a comfortable life but an important job to do and one he took seriously. Every day, he sat at the window on guard duty, always alert and ready to bark at anyone who lingered too long in front of the house.

But one bright, sunny day, Pierre did the unthinkable. He left his post!

He crept away from his house, inching his way to freedom, turning around to make sure no one could catch him.

When Pierre reached the end of the street, he took a final look back and turned the corner. With his head held high and ears back, his white fur fluffed by a light breeze, Pierre broke into a trot and hit the open road where boundless possibilities awaited him. I swear he was smiling.

Where did Pierre find the courage to leave his comfortable spot? Was it a whim? Was it a repressed longing that finally exploded within him? Did a little voice say, "Find your inner wild. Go ahead. Do it!"?

I hope so.

What is wild, anyway? Untamed and out of control. *But* it's also passionate and fierce.

Have we been so thoroughly domesticated that cautiousness rules, making life dull and predictable?

Wouldn't it be exciting to unleash our inner wild on an open road with the wind in our hair and the sun on our face?

JOY

Sail into the Wind

The morning sky glows with a mix of bright-pink and blue-tinted clouds. The heavens are expecting twins.

In the morning's hush, before the day's rush, the trees quiver in anticipation of the birth.

The skylight softens as she delivers the day along with childhood memories of daydreaming beneath the shade of a red maple tree on sultry, summer days. I would tuck myself into the perfect hollow between the roots poking up through the ground and watch a parade of clouds created just for me.

Now I sit under the outstretched branches of a shade tree as the sky pushes fluffy clouds from their hiding place behind the green hills.

An angel blowing a trumpet announces the beginning of the cloud parade. A puppy running through the grass is next, followed by a kitten playing with its paws and then a man smoking a pipe.

Then the clouds gather and form an ocean where a baby dolphin frolics in the waves next to an enormous ship. On its bow is a figurehead, not a man, woman, or animal, but a creature with a mass of wavy hair, unlike anything I've ever seen before.

The ship slows down.

"Where do you want to go?" the creature asks me.

"On an adventure to somewhere I've never been before," I reply as I climb aboard.

The creature, one bright eye shining, grins as we sail into the wind.

DANCE YOUR DANCE

My beautiful catbird, dressed in her sophisticated sleek gray suit and little black cap, makes her entrance onto the garden shed's roof.

Sunlight streams through the opening in the leafy canopy of trees and fixes a spotlight on the tiny pool of water below. My catbird pauses. Then with a delicate flutter, she descends to perch on the edge of the birdbath.

My elegant bird takes a few dainty sips of water and then wades into the pool. Cocking her head from side to side, she waits and listens for the dance music only she can hear.

Once my catbird hears her cue, she dunks her head under the water and quickly stands upright. She pauses and then gracefully lowers her whole body into the water. Suddenly, she spreads her wings and breaks into her exuberant dance of flaps, flutters, and splashes with dazzling abandon. She is free like the wildflowers that pop up in the most unlikely places.

My beautiful little bird dances for herself, without worrying how it's supposed to be done or about pleasing anyone else. Her flutters sprinkle waterdrops that shimmer in the sun and bring joy to her heart and mine.

WINTER'S LAST VISIT

A mist of March snow catches the azaleas by surprise, dusting their new leaves. Crocuses that popped up all happy purple probably wish they hadn't been so eager to greet spring.

Blades of grass shiver under its icy coat. Bamboo leaves tremble as they surrender to winter's coating of cold, wet flakes.

Defiant tulip leaves stand stiff and dare the snow to linger on them. Not wanting a fight, the snow moves on.

Oak trees that have endured many winters don't mind this last snow. They allow it to settle into the crooks where their limbs meet their trunks and snag on their craggy, grizzled bodies.

The pines and holly trees love winter's last visit and its gift of a bright-white winter coat.

A bird stands on a slender branch. I wonder if it will open its beak to catch snowflakes before flying off to play.

WINTER'S PINCH

Naked tree branches rest against the pale winter sky. Everything seems drab, dreary, or dead.

But brilliant red cardinals and holly berries dot the earth like exclamation points.

Frosty air tickles my nose until I surrender and breathe in winter's purity until my lungs can't hold anymore.

Snowflakes dance until they are dizzy and fall to the ground like children who have spun too long and too fast.

Icicles shed one crystalline drop at a time in magical slow motion.

Pines wrap themselves in forest-green coats and stand warm and happy in the snow.

Below the cold, crusted earth, turnips and carrots hide, sucking up the soil's flavor so they taste earthy and sweet.

Winter makes my eyes water and my nose run. It numbs my fingers and toes. Winter lovingly pinches my cheeks and asks, "Without me, how will you know you are truly alive?"

Night Rain

Night is nearly over. Daylight hasn't arrived, but the rain has.

It taps on the window, softly. It doesn't want to wake me, but my eyes are already open.

The room is dark and I can't see anything. I take sips of air so nothing, not even the sound of my breathing, interrupts the pure, singular sound of rain.

It plays a song for me, a comforting drumbeat on the roof that becomes a liquid melody spilling to the sleeping flowers that wait below.

Thunder and lightning intrude on us. Don't they know that we prefer to be alone, the rain and I?

The rain becomes a drizzle, hoping it can lull me back to sleep. But I don't want to leave the rain.

I rest quietly under a soft blanket until daylight peeks around the edges of the window blind and tells me it's time to get up. I open the shades.

The rain continues, but its spell is broken. Rain doesn't sound the same in the gray light of day.

CICADA CHORUS

Hot, sticky weather has driven me inside for too many summer days. I am grateful for a cool house, but tonight I need to escape the mechanical whirr of the air conditioner.

I sit on the screened porch, away from hungry mosquitoes. Just as I settle in to enjoy the quiet and watch the birds play in the birdbath, cicadas decide to join me.

They arrive like drunken guests at a party, loud and insistent, with a high-pitched whine that pierces my peace.

Why can't they go away or at least stop making that monstrous noise?

But they don't. They happily continue their irritating shrill drone.

The cacophony grows louder and grates on my nerves.

I can't stand this clamor anymore; I'm going inside. But then the cicadas surprise me.

They begin to hum a soft, smooth note. The altos begin the verse and the sopranos join in on the refrain. Then the low voices fall silent, the sopranos carry the melody to a crescendo, and then all hum in harmony to the end.

As soon as the cicadas finish one song, they begin another, never waiting for applause.

Their recital is now a soothing mellifluous chorus that serenades on a sultry summer night.

Did the cicadas change, or did I?

MOON BUNNY

Night has fallen. Mother Nature pulls her cozy deepest blue blanket over the sky and tells everyone to go to sleep.

But as soon as she's gone, the little ones turn on their flashlights, lighting up the sky with twinkly stars. Some of them slip behind the bare branches of trees, playing hide-and-seek, giggling, because I can't find them.

The luminous full moon hugs a bunny with a fluffy cotton-ball tail and ears that stand up like flags in the wind.

The bunny loves to cuddle, but he is eager to play so he wriggles free from the moon. He hops all over the heavens, playing with his starry friends for a long time. Sometimes I see him and other times, the bunny hides from me.

Then Mama Moon decides it's time for her little bunny to come in to rest for a while. When she calls, he runs home to her. Mama Moon wraps him in her loving arms and says, "Hush now, and go to sleep. Then you can go back out to play."

The bunny settles into his comfortable nest and presses his nose against the bubble of the moon, watching his starry playmates until his eyes flutter shut in dreamy sleep.

BEACH TOYS

Shells are scattered everywhere on the beach like a child's toys.

I stoop to pluck the colorful, unusual, and pretty from their sandy nest. Some are easily found gleaming on the shore. Others are buried. Some are whole shells. Others are slivers. But all are treasures in Mother Nature's toy chest.

I hold the sun-warmed shells as if I were stroking the hair of a well-loved doll. The ridged and bumpy shells become the eyes, noses, and mouths of wrinkled funny faces grinning at me. Curlicue shells that hide rocks in their crevices fascinate me like a puzzle I can't quite figure out. Shells in all shades of yellows, oranges, purples, and browns make me happy like a giant box of brand-new crayons.

Concave shells are perfect shovels that mound piles of sand into forts and castles for a princess. Swirly spiral shapes wrapped with bronze and ivory raised beads decorate their turrets. Flat purple shells line the roads to the castles' gates.

I wonder why some are thick and craggy while others are so tiny and delicate I can't imagine how they survive being tumbled about in the gritty salt water.

But does a child really need to know how her toys are made?

Ocean in My Hand

I'm bundled up in a warm house, but I still feel this six-degree day deep in my bones.

My fingers search the small bag of seashells on my desk, hoping they can work their warming magic. A broken shell chooses me. It fits perfectly in my palm.

I curl my hand around it and feel the underside that is full of subtle ridges and indentations, like the peaks and valleys of the ocean's floor.

Colorful bands of cream and charcoal that stretch across the shell's face remind me of the endless ebb and flow of the ocean's waves.

A lacy pattern of tiny holes on the shell's edge look like the frothy bubbles at the end of each ocean wave that dance for a moment and then disappear.

This wave I hold in my hand carries me to summer and the beach where wet sand tugs at my feet as the throbbing sun warms my skin. I can hear the whoosh of waves and the squawks of swooping gulls that call to each other. When I bring the shell close, I smell salty fresh air and forget the cold, wet gray day.

Then, I find one more surprise. In this eternal wave in my hand, I see the rounded back and blunt-tipped nose of a dolphin caught in its early-morning swim slipping gracefully in and out of the water as its body glistens under the rising sun.

CHRISTMAS RICHES

I was promised a very special Christmas gift this year. In the early-morning sky, a full moon would appear on Christmas Day for the first time in thirty-eight years. There wouldn't be another one on this day for nineteen more years.

I woke up early, excited. But my moon present wasn't there! Instead, milky gray clouds covered the sky and pushed the moon away. I was so disappointed that I couldn't have the one gift I really wanted.

But I wasn't going to give up. There was one last chance for the Christmas moon to appear. When Christmas night arrived, I was hopeful and excited but prepared to be disappointed.

But there it was. A magnificent full Christmas moon beamed brightly for me. The best present ever.

The jealous clouds couldn't stand that they weren't the center of attention so they swept in and surrounded the moon. I guess they thought they had won, but they couldn't hide my gift.

Instead, the Christmas moon glowed among the clouds like a coin slipping through the slot in a piggy bank.

What if the moon were a big, bright shiny coin?

Then we'd be fabulously rich.

Twinkles in the Night

The sun's high beams kick up smoking heat and send blinding white light everywhere you look. Summer's bounty of ripe fruit and vegetables bursts out of gardens. Thunderstorms boom and jagged bolts of lightning slash ominous skies.

Big, old flashy summer is here, and she will not be ignored.

So who could blame us if we overlook the lightning bugs flying in slow motion as the sun sinks in the sky? Silently, their bodies blink on and off, on and off, in the sticky humid air, pinholes of light in twilight's curtain.

As a child, I would beg my mother for a glass jar, one that, despite being washed, always retained the distinctive scent of pickles. I poked holes in the top so the captured lightning bugs could breathe. I lined it with grass so they would be comfortable.

Even though I was a curious child, it never occurred to me to ask why these bugs blinked. Their luminescence enthralled me.

I would tiptoe up to the lightning bugs, capturing one at a time. Trapping a new bug without releasing any of the ones already in captivity was an art form. And I was good at it. My goal was to fill the entire jar, but I rarely caught more than three at a time.

Before I went to sleep, I would place the jar by my bed, hoping that my little friends would flick on and off, illuminating my room all night. But I was always disappointed.

Maybe they were upset that they couldn't roam free or

they missed their friends. Perhaps they didn't like the pickle-scented jar. Maybe they were frustrated that I had interrupted their search for a sweetheart. Turns out those blinks are winks meant to attract a mate.

Maybe my punishment for their capture was to turn off their lights. But I don't think that's what happened.

My companions still blinked on and off, but one pulse of light on its own in a closed pickle jar can be missed. It takes a blink — one here, one there, another and another, all together twinkling in the night sky — that creates magic.

DANCE IN MY MOONBEAMS

Tonight, a panda bear plays in the balloon of my moon. I've seen hills, valleys, a bunny, and occasionally a man in the moon before, but never, ever a panda bear.

Tonight, though, is special.

Do you know they've named you Super Moon because you are bigger and brighter than you've been in a long time? That's funny because I think you're always a super moon.

You are nearer to me tonight than usual, but couldn't you come a little closer? My fingertips can't quite reach your smiling face and the panda bear within you.

I don't know, and I'd like you to tell me, please, Moon: Are you soft and squishy like a marshmallow, or dusty like talcum powder, or cool and smooth like granite?

Silly me. I know what you're made of.

You're a downy, warm pillow in the snug cradle of the sky where you catch all my sweet dreams and tuck them in so they are safe and won't get lost in the dark. Maybe that's why somehow I'm less lonely when I see you looking down on me from the night sky.

Now you are full to bursting with all of my dreams. They bubble up around the panda, tickle his nose, and make him giggle.

"Dance in my moonbeams. They are full of your dreams," the moon says to me. "They are ready now, and so are you."

I open my arms as I twirl round and round to receive my

bright and shining hopes bundled with your loving wishes that all my dreams come true.

I know, Moon, it's time for you to go. But before you do, please sprinkle some dream dust across the sky in the form of stars to remind me to dream a thousand more dreams and fill you up once again.

ACKNOWLEDGMENTS

Writing a book is a solitary pursuit, but one I did not have to chase alone. I'm grateful to my first writing teacher, Elizabeth Ayres, whose innovative approach to teaching helped me get the words flowing and rediscover the joy of writing. Beverly Down gently encouraged me to share my writing with an audience and wouldn't take no for an answer.

I'm grateful to five women who walked the publishing road before me. Liane Young, good friend and author, offered helpful comments about the book and publishing advice. Stacia Fleegal stuck with me, editing many drafts over several years. Andi Cumbo-Floyd, whose blog inspires me, introduced me to Shayla Raquel, who edited, proofed, and patiently guided me toward publication. Melinda Martin did a wonderful job on the cover design and interior formatting.

Many thanks to all the classmates in workshops and retreats with me who read and provided thoughtful comments on my work. I'm grateful to all my friends for their enthusiastic support of this project.

Thanks to my sister, Ann, who loves and supports me in all I do.

And finally, to my husband, Richard, who always believed in my writing ability. I treasure the beautiful desk you built for me where I do all my writing. I'm grateful for all the times you cooked, listened, and read drafts through the long process of creating *Nature's Quiet Wisdom*. Your encouragement, suggestions, insight, care, and, most of all, your love mean the world to me.

ABOUT THE AUTHOR

LYNN H. WYVILL grew up in Washington DC where her favorite activity was sitting under a Japanese red maple tree, watching clouds create pictures in the sky. As a writer, she finds peace and inspiration when hiking in the woods, strolling on sandy beaches, and observing nature's show in her backyard. Those experiences are captured in her first book, *Nature's Quiet Wisdom*. Before writing books, Lynn worked as a radio/TV reporter and writer for the US Department of Agriculture and owned a consulting business that trained professionals on the creation and delivery of effective presentations. She is a lifelong learner, avid reader, small town explorer, and dedicated theater attendee who lives in beautiful Virginia with her husband.

CONNECT WITH THE AUTHOR

LynnHWyvill.com
lynn@lynnhwyvill.com

LEAVE A REVIEW

If you enjoyed this book, will you please consider writing a review on Amazon and Goodreads? Reviews help self-published authors make their books more visible to new readers.

64806911R10054

Made in the USA
Middletown, DE
31 August 2019